Hello, Family Members,

Learning to read is one of the most important accomplishments of early childhood. **Hello Reader!** books are designed to help children become skilled readers who like to read. Beginning readers learn to read by remembering frequently used words like "the," "is," and "and"; by using phonics skills to decode new words; and by interpreting picture and text clues. These books provide both the stories children enjoy and the structure they need to read fluently and independently. Here are suggestions for helping your child *before, during,* and *after* reading:

Before

- Look at the cover and pictures and have your child predict what the story is about.
- Read the story to your child.
- Encourage your child to chime in with familiar words and phrases.
- Echo read with your child by reading a line first and having your child read it after you do.

During

- Have your child think about a word he or she does not recognize right away. Provide hints such as "Let's see if we know the sounds" and "Have we read other words like this one?"
- Encourage your child to use phonics skills to sound out new words.
- Provide the word for your child when more assistance is needed so that he or she does not struggle and the experience of reading with you is a positive one.
- Encourage your child to have fun by reading with a lot of expression . . . like an actor!

After

- Have your child keep lists of interesting and favorite words.
- Encourage your child to read the books over and over again. Have him or her read to brothers, sisters, grandparents, and even teddy-bears. Repeated readings develop confidence in young readers.
- Talk about the stories. Ask and answer questions. Share ideas about the funniest and most interesting characters and events in the stories.

I do hope that you and your child enjoy this book.

—Francie Alexander
　Reading Specialist,
　Scholastic's Learning Ventures

For Jack and Selma, with love
— M.B.

Special thanks to Laurie Roulston
of the Denver Museum of Natural History
for her expertise

Text copyright © 2000 by Melvin Berger.

Photography and illustration credits:

Cover: Norbert Wu; page 3 and 12: Gregory Ochocki/Innerspace Visions, courtesy of Scripps Institution of Oceanography; page 4: Dale Stokes/Mo Yung Productions; page 7: Norbert Wu; page 8: Gregory Ochocki/Innerspace Visions, courtesy of Scripps Institution of Oceanography; pages 10-11, 13-16: Norbert Wu; page 18: Doug Perrine/Innerspace Visions; page 19: Bob Cranston/Innerspace Visions; page 20: James D. Watt/Innerspace Visions; page 21: Bob Cranston/Innerspace Visions; pages 22-24: Richard Ellis/Innerspace Visions; page 27: Michael S. Nolan/Innerspace Visions; page 28: Doug Perrine/Innerspace Visions; pages 30-32: Norbert Wu; page 34: David Fleetham/Innerspace Visions; page 35: Doug Perrine/Innerspace Visions; page 36: Andrew J. Martinez/Photo Researchers; page 37: B. Murton/Southampton Oceanography Centre/Science Photo Library/Photo Researchers; page 38: 1993 NSF Oasis Project/Norbert Wu; page 40: Norbert Wu.

Library of Congress Cataloging-in-Publication Data

Berger, Melvin.
    Dive! : a book of deep sea creatures / by Melvin Berger.
        p.   cm. — (Hello reader! Science. Level 3)
    Summary: Uses a submarine trip to the bottom of the sea to introduce various deep-sea creatures, including the angler fish, octopus, and sperm whale.
    ISBN: 0-439-08747-3
    1. Deep-sea animals —Juvenile literature.   [1. Marine animals.]   I. Title. II. Series.
QL125.5 .B47   2000
591.77'7 21—dc21

99-042690

12 11 10 9 8 7 6 5 4 3 2 1

00 01 02 03 04 05 06

Printed in the U.S.A.
First printing, March 2000

23

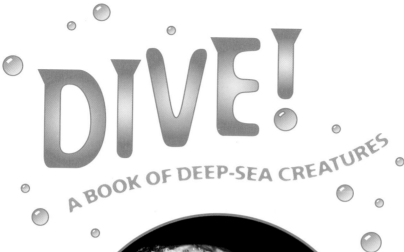

DIVE!
A BOOK OF DEEP-SEA CREATURES

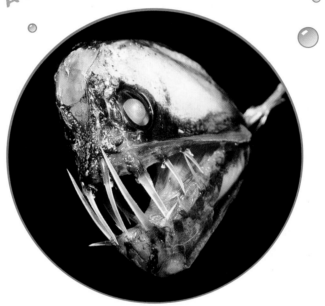

by Melvin Berger

Hello Reader! Science — Level 3

SCHOLASTIC INC. Cartwheel B·O·O·K·S®

New York Toronto London Auckland Sydney
Mexico City New Delhi Hong Kong

CHAPTER ONE

Down to the Bottom

Would you like to visit the bottom
of the sea?
It's easy.
Just climb aboard a little submarine.
Take your seat — and let's go!

The submarine dives down below
the surface.
At first the water is bright blue.
It sparkles in the sunlight.
There are many fish.

As the submarine drops deeper
and deeper, the water gets very dark.
The sun's rays don't reach this far.
Fewer fish swim here.

Finally, the submarine is one mile
under the sea.
The water is darker than
the darkest night.

BUMP!
The submarine lands on the ocean bottom
and shines a bright light.
The sea floor is muddy.
It's covered with fish bones and
broken shells.
The water, if you could feel it,
is freezing cold.

Very few plants and animals live here.

How odd they look!

Like beings from another planet.

Welcome to the weird and wonderful

world of deep-sea creatures!

CHAPTER TWO

Flashing Lights

The sea is black.
But look closely and you'll see tiny lights
darting this way and that.

The lights come from animals that
live here.
Most of these animals make their own
light from chemicals inside their bodies.
The light acts like bait.
It attracts prey, or other creatures,
which the animals like to eat.

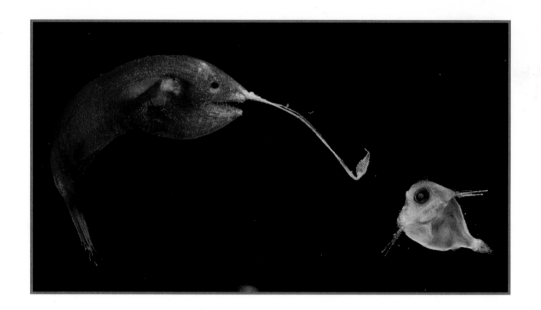

The **angler fish** lives near the bottom
of the ocean.
The female has a long rod that hangs
from her head.
It looks like a fishing pole.
But instead of a worm at the end,
the pole has a light.

Other fish swim toward the light.
When one gets close, the angler fish
snatches it in her mouth.
Good-bye fish!

The angler fish has something else
on her head.
It's the much, much smaller male
angler fish!
He attaches himself to her.
And he stays there for the rest of his life.
A very close couple!

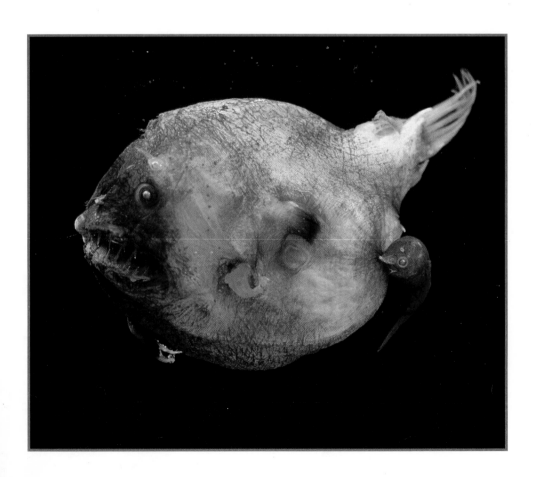

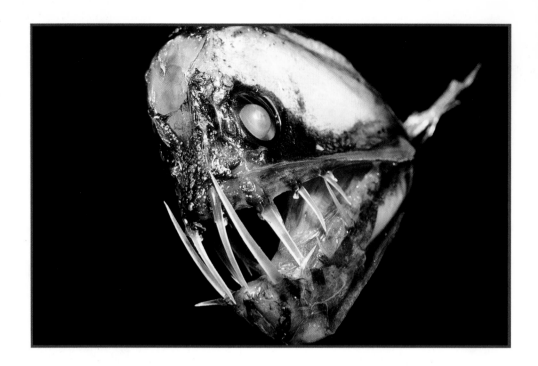

Viper fish dangle an outside light
like angler fish.
But some viper fish have extra lights.
These lights are *inside* the mouth!

The viper fish swims with its mouth
open wide.
The lights attract small fish.
They head for the bright spots.
Before you know it, the hungry viper fish
gulps down the fish.

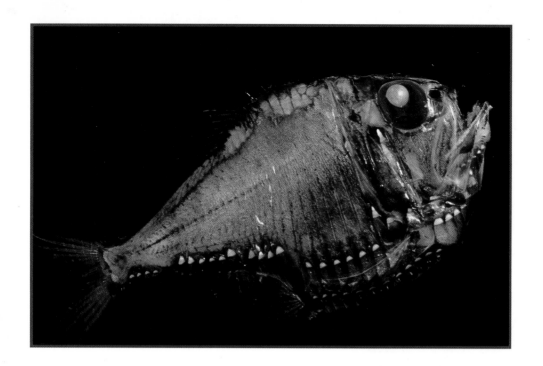

The **hatchet fish** has no light on a pole.
Instead, rows of light line the bottom
of its body.
The lights sparkle as the hatchet fish
swims.

Some fish rush over to get a better look.
That's a mistake.
The hatchet fish twists around with jaws
wide open.
In one bite, the fish swallows its prey.

Flashlight fish also give off light.
But they don't make the light themselves.
The light comes from glowing germs,
or bacteria, inside their body.

Flashlight fish have two see-through bags
under their eyes.
That's where the glowing bacteria live.
The fish cannot switch off the bacteria.
But they can cover them with a layer
of skin.

The light helps protect the flashlight fish.
Suppose it sees an enemy.
The flashlight fish swims in a straight line
with lights on.
Then it covers them up.

Quickly the flashlight fish turns.
Surprise!
The enemy can't find it.
The fish swims safely away.

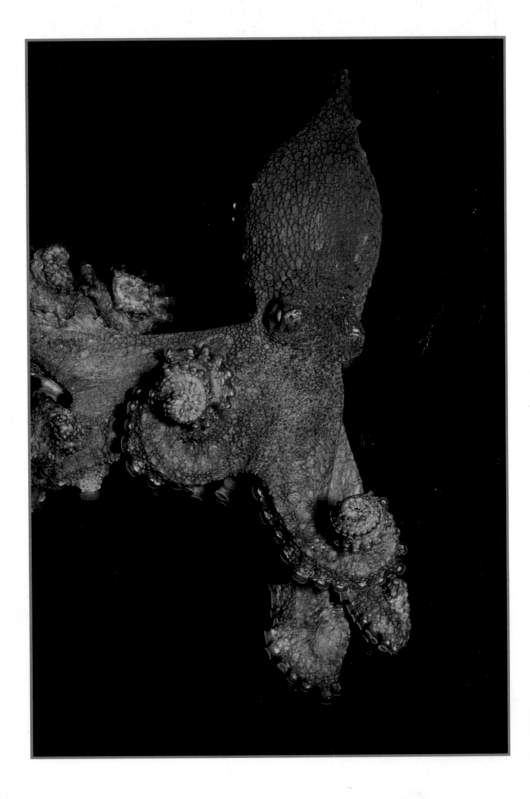

CHAPTER THREE

Huge Eyes and Wagging Arms

Many deep-sea creatures have
huge eyes.
Can you guess why?
The bigger their eyes, the better they
can see in the dark.

Certain **octopuses** live in very
deep water.
They have two great, big eyes that
help them spot their prey.

Eight arms stretch out from the head of an octopus.
Each arm has two rows of small, round suckers.
They can grab and hold anything.
If an octopus loses an arm, a new one grows in its place.

Squid are like octopuses.

Each has two gigantic eyes.

Around a squid's head are ten arms —

eight long ones plus two extra-long ones.

The arms have suckers to catch prey.

A squid swims in an odd way.
It fills parts of its body with water and
then forces the water out.
This shoots the squid forward, much like
a jet plane.

When the squid spots a fish's lights,
it whips out its arms.
The arms trap the fish.
The squid pops the fish into its mouth.

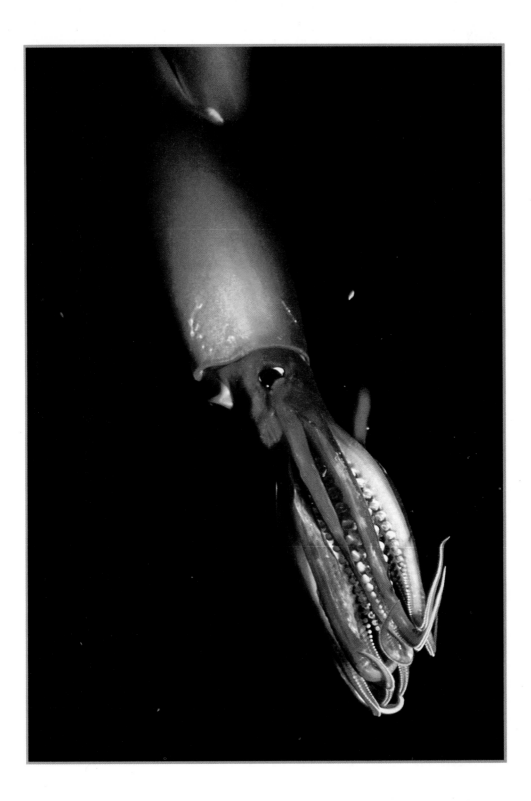

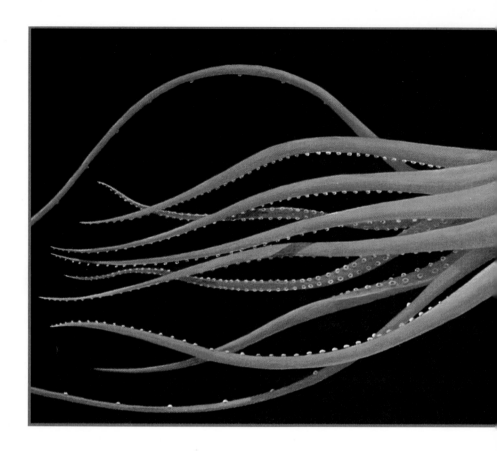

The **giant squid** is the largest squid
of all.
Its body can grow longer than
a big bus!

This dark red deep-sea creature has
the largest eyes of any animal on earth.
Each is the size of a car's hubcap!

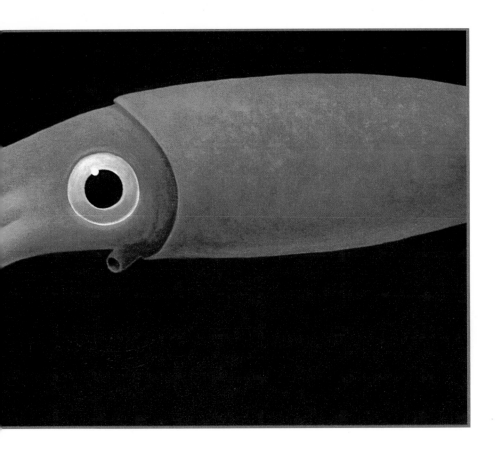

The squid's tongue is not for licking.
Its tongue has teeth!
The squid uses it for chewing.

Sailors used to tell of huge monsters
that lived in the sea.
Now we think those monsters were
really giant squid!

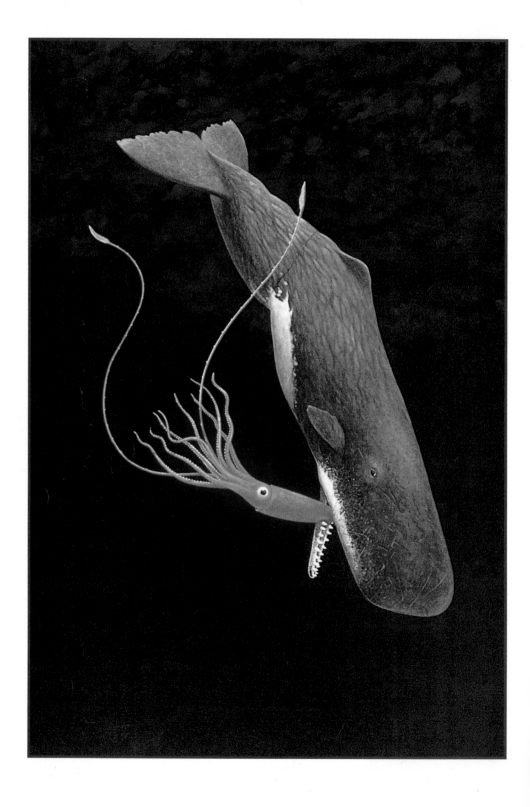

CHAPTER FOUR

Deep-sea Diver

The giant squid fears only one deep-sea animal — the mighty **sperm whale**. This whale eats many different sea creatures. But its favorite is the giant squid.

The sperm whale is like other whales. It goes up to the surface to breathe air. Yet it also feeds on squid at the ocean bottom. How does the sperm whale do this? It's a deep-sea diver!

The sperm whale first fills its huge lungs
with air.
Then it holds its breath and plunges down,
head first.
After a mile or so, the whale comes to rest
on the ocean floor.
It stops and waits.

If the whale is lucky, a giant squid swims by.
The whale slams its mouth shut
on one of the squid's arms.
The squid puts up a fight.

The whale and the squid are about the
same length.
But the whale is much heavier.
It swallows the squid in one gulp —
whole and alive!
But the squid keeps on fighting.
It cuts and scratches the whale's stomach
leaving scars inside.

A sperm whale can only stay in deep
water for about an hour.
Then it needs to breathe.
The whale swims to the surface
and breathes out.
Its warm breath forms a mist
that sprays up like a fountain.

After a while, the whale takes another
deep breath.
And down it plunges.

CHAPTER FIVE

Big Mouths and Elastic Stomachs

Life is hard in deep water.
It can be a long time between meals.
Once in a great while, there's lots to eat.
Then the fish want to gobble up
all they can.
Large mouths and elastic stomachs are
a big help.

Fish near the ocean bottom are
usually small.
But many have mouths that can open
real wide.
Their jaws swing far apart.
They can swallow prey twice their size!

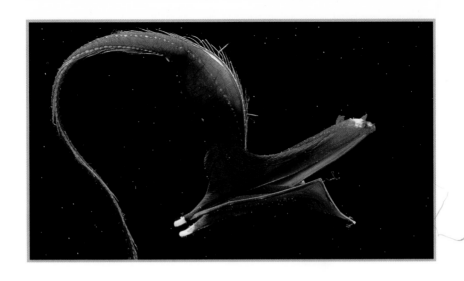

The mouth of the **gulper eel** is the biggest part of its body.
The rest is long and thin like a tail.
A small, red light at the end looks like a taillight on a car.

The taillight attracts prey.
The jaws take care of the rest.
Dozens of small, sharp teeth hold the victim.
Then the gulper swallows it whole.

As the gulper eats, its belly grows larger and larger.
It can double in size!

The **great swallower** also has a huge mouth and an elastic stomach.
You can guess how it got its name.
It's only about six inches long.
Yet this fish can swallow prey almost twice its size.

Sometimes the great swallower stuffs itself with food.
The skin over its belly stretches very thin.
Look closely and you can see its last meal inside!

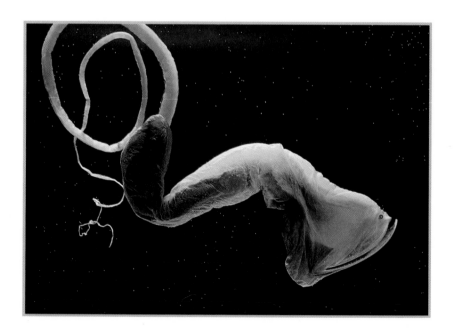

CHAPTER SIX

The Ocean Floor

The ocean floor has few signs of life.
But the creatures that do live here are
very strange.
Most bizarre is the **tripod fish**.
It walks!

The tripod walks on three "legs" —
its two stiff side fins and tail.
They lift the fish off the ocean floor.
Best of all, they let it catch shrimp that
swim just above the ocean bottom.

The **ratfish** looks a little like a shark.
It digs in the mud for creatures that
hide there.
Sometimes it finds bits of food buried
in the ooze.

Male ratfish attract females
in an odd way.
They make loud drumming sounds.
If a female likes the beat, she swims over.

Sea cucumbers look like garden cucumbers with legs.
But they're animals, not vegetables.
These tubby creatures live in large groups.
In the mud, they find what they like to eat.

Fish and crabs prey on sea cucumbers.
But these enemies had better watch out.
When in danger, sea cucumbers squirt out long, sticky tubes.
The tubes tangle up the enemy.
And they give the sea cucumber a chance to escape.

Sea pens are like sea cucumbers. Large numbers live together on the ocean floor. Each sea pen looks like an old-fashioned quill or feather pen. Rooted to one spot, they wait to have their food delivered. Each snatches small bits of food from the water around it.

Also stuck in the sea floor are **sea squirts**. Their name comes from the way they take in water, pull out any tiny creatures, and squirt out the rest of the water.

CHAPTER SEVEN

Black Smokers

Deep water is icy cold — except in
a very few places.

Here, cold water seeps down
through cracks in the ocean floor.
The heat inside the earth warms
the water.

The warm water bubbles up through
"chimneys," called black smokers.

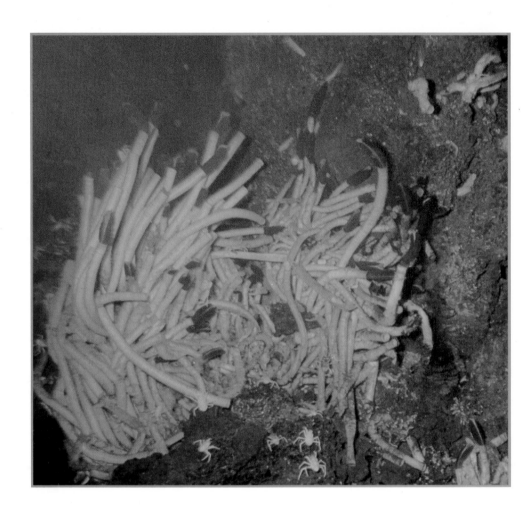

Tubeworms cluster around these
warm spots.
The creatures live inside tall, thin,
white tubes stuck to the ocean floor.
They make the tubes from sand
and material from their own bodies.

The tubes protect them from crabs
and other enemies.
The tallest are about the height
of a tall man.
Tubeworms don't have to look for food.
Bacteria in their body make food
for them.
The bacteria get chemicals
from the water around the smokers.
The chemicals feed the bacteria,
which become food for the tubeworms.

Deep-sea shrimp also count on bacteria
for food.
These bacteria live in their mouth.
They take in chemicals that the shrimp
scrapes loose from the ocean floor.
The chemicals feed the bacteria,
which become food for the shrimp.

Even a submarine can't stay underwater forever.

It's time to leave the deep-sea creatures with —

- flashing lights,
- huge eyes and wagging arms,
- big mouths and elastic stomachs,
- three "legs," and
- bodies stuck in the mud.

Let's hope we see them again soon!